SEGOvIA
my book of the guitar

guidance for the beginner

SEGOVIA
my book of the guitar

BY ANDRÉS SEGOVIA AND GEORGE MENDOZA

creative designer nicole sekora-mendoza

photographer gerhard gscheidle

PHILOMEL BOOKS

NEW YORK

acknowledgements

My most profound thanks to all who believed in and would not extinguish the brilliant *fanion* of my stubborn dream :

Marquesa de Saavedra
who first introduced us to Maestro Andrés Segovia
Jesús Silva
pupil of Andrés Segovia and one of the world's leading classical guitarists, who created the studies, melodies and little pieces for the *lessons*
Alexandre Tansman
the internationally noted composer, for his musical contribution
Vladimir Bobri
Editor, *The Guitar Review,* who extended both helping hands
Joan Clibbon
of *Collins,* London
Ann Beneduce
of *Collins,* New York
Michel Duplaix
of *Flammarion,* Paris
Michael Dadap and **Juan Orozco**
who helped in the preparation of the project
Iberia Airlines
Enrique Garcia Herraiz
of the *Spanish National Tourist Office,* New York
Pablo Kessler
Director, *Hotel Ritz,* Madrid, who allowed Ashley and Ryan to take over the prestigious hotel for several weeks, including their selling of penny candies in the grand hotel lobby between guitar sessions
and especially to **Maestro Andrés Segovia** and my wife, Nicole, "tyrant" as Maestro tenderly called her, who both seemed to work together like the musical flow of the moon with the tide, my feelings of gratitude can never truly be expressed because they already know my commitment and love... — G.M.

other credits : photograph by Michel Duplaix, p. 9; pastel drawing of Segovia by English painter, Mr. Palmer, 1919, p. 11; pencil drawing by international painter, D. Manuel Rivera, back cover; photographs courtesy Vladimir Bobri, pgs. 12, 13, 26 (Segovia), 27 and 30.

In remembrance of my early age,
when I had to toil trying to learn
how to play
the classical guitar by myself,
I offer here
a few exercises and observations
for further technical development
to the student
with no access to competent instruction.

Andrés Segovia

contents

introduction by george mendoza

Sympathetic Insistence...This book opened before you now with a mere flick of your finger was not an easy task to realize. Indeed, it was more like climbing the sheer rock side of a mountain after crossing a turbulent stream in full spate. A seemingly endless labor of love, it took nearly three years of countless trips to Spain, letters, and long distance phone conversations to convince Maestro Segovia that he should work with me to produce such a work. But most of all, it required patience, for it must be understood that I was asking a genius to divert himself from the set course of his work and life, to spare time to give guidance to you, the beginner of the classical guitar.

I'm sure you can well imagine how many writers and publishers have pursued the Maestro over the years, asking him to convey his knowledge of the guitar into print form so that beginners might have a glimpse of his method, his technique.

How then, you surely must ask, did Andrés Segovia come finally to doing this book? Maestro said it was because of my "sympathetic insistence." But it was more, I know, much more. Looking back, I remember those great waves of Maestro Segovia's caution and reluctance to say yes, I will work with you. His primary concern was that he did not want to be part of a rigidly didactic teaching experience, and rightly so. So, when I diffidently suggested that he teach my two children, Ryan and Ashley, ages six and nine, children just beginning to take an interest in the guitar, his first reaction was a wide smile — however, I was not sure if this indicated irony or pleasure. But then, suddenly, I felt myself swept into his rarefied world. He accepted the idea of working directly with the children, and thus creating a book from a center of warmth and love — not from the cold and impersonal winds of facts and method alone.

And so, for the first time, the master, Andrés Segovia, will share with you in this book the principles of his unsurpassed technique. You will touch his wisdoms and his spirit as you pluck through his music and read Segovia's words (which appear italicized throughout the book) and you will come to feel, as I did, a sense of his rare humanity and his particular genius, beyond what the Spanish call — *duende*.

G.M.

Paris — 1978

The sun illuminates only the eye of the man,
but shines into the eye and the heart of the child.
                              Ralph Waldo Emerson

the road from my birth to the first concert i gave

In several dictionaries you may read different dates concerning where and when I was born.

However, I suppose that no musical archeologist will ever fight with another in order to establish in the future the exactness of that point. The truth is that I came to this world the 21st day of February in the year 1893 in Linares, a small and charming village belonging to the Andalusian province of Jaén.

Observe, please, this remarkable coincidence, maybe the root of my destiny : there was at the door of the next house, a very important guitar shop. Euterpe, the goddess of music, put into my soul the seed of that marvelous and mysterious Art. She guided the development of that gift with benevolence, although I was somewhat ungrateful to her, because instead of taking the flute, instrument ascribed to her, I chose the guitar. But she was not angry, demonstrating by that her good taste and her broad indulgence.

My family took me to Granada where I opened my eyes to the world of beauty. Having no teacher there from whom I could learn the technique of the guitar, I decided to name myself both pupil and master.

The pupil was a passionate ignorant, and the master, under the fire of my questions, less than an ignorant…Nevertheless, we did not quarrel too much, and this association has lasted until the present time…

I gave my first concert, pushed to the stage by my kind friends in the Centro Artistico of Granada. —I was sixteen years old. When I read the generous review of my concert in the small newspaper of the city, I thought, ingenuously, that I was already famous throughout the whole world.

The Guitar
      to Andrés Segovia

Sonorous eight where the air waits asleep
for the awakening of harmony,
strings taut and tense, still carrying silently
the glory hidden in their secret keep,

fingerboard on whose black, elegant sweep
strings and frets weave in strict geometry
a hexagram, now quiet, that presently
will come alive with music — from the deep

of your circumference, sonorous eight,
a hand by genius led will recreate
of Johann Sebastian Bach the melody,

assailing heaven with a mighty stream
of golden voices mustered in a dream
of scales of an unfailing symmetry.

            Salvador de Madariaga

the guitar
and parts

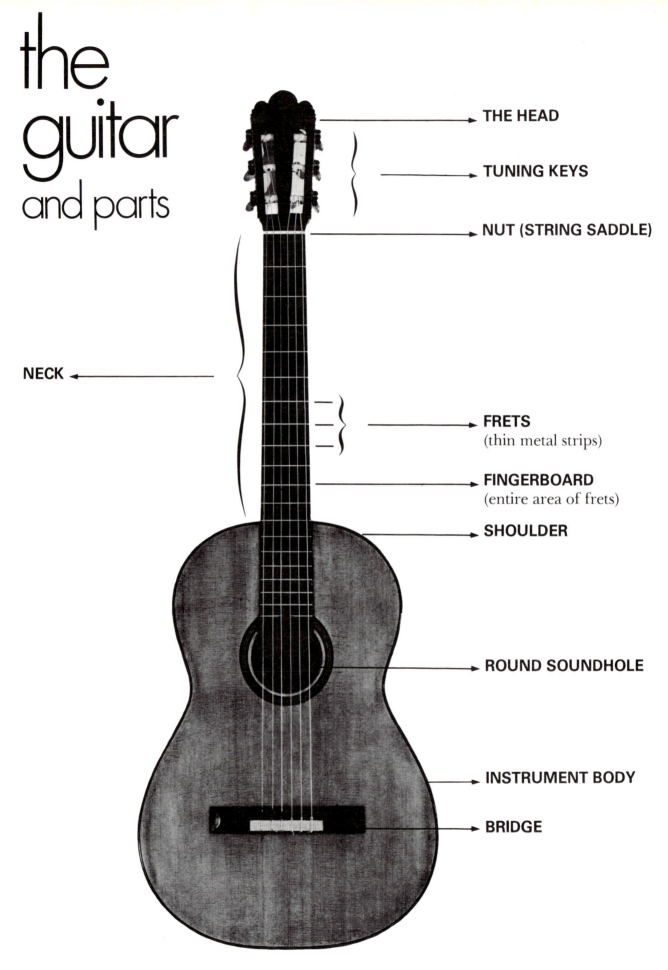

THE HEAD

TUNING KEYS

NUT (STRING SADDLE)

NECK

FRETS
(thin metal strips)

FINGERBOARD
(entire area of frets)

SHOULDER

ROUND SOUNDHOLE

INSTRUMENT BODY

BRIDGE

Guitar by Antonio Torres, 1863.
Collection Rose L. Augustine

I like the sound of the guitar...

the guitar

I will tell you something about the origin of the guitar. The conclusions of recent investigations are : the Greek Lyra, *whose case of resonance was shaped like a tortoise, was the source of such instruments as the lute, the mandolin and the violin. The* Cithar, *younger than the* Lyra, *whose case was flat and with sides, was the origin of the guitar. If you pronounce the* C *like* K, *you obtain* Kitar = Guitar. *Up to now, this is arid, historical data.*

But the following legend is more beautiful and poetical :

Apollo saw Cupid, the son of Venus, a mischievous and naughty boy, and scolded him saying, "You are too young to play with your bow and arrows." Cupid was very much displeased with these words. Resentful, he shot an arrow to the heart of Apollo who instantly felt the fire of a devastating love for Daphne, the beautiful nymph who happened to be passing by. And Cupid shot another arrow to the heart of Daphne to kindle in it an aversion to love.

Apollo ran after her and when she finally fell into his arms, she invoked the help of her father, who was also a demigod. He converted her into a tree, the Laurel, *which in Greek is called Daphne.*

Apollo made the first guitar from that spendid tree, and with its leaves we crown the great poets and artists. The guitar preserves from its feminine origin the curved lines of her body, and also the tendency of becoming very often whimsical and unpredictable.

rudiments of music

Learning to read music is like learning a different language, but instead of only words, the language of music consists of symbols, and signs, and terms that have their own special meanings. The *rudiments of music* serve as the solid foundation upon which all music is built. It is therefore essential that you begin to comprehend music in an orderly step-by-step fashion, for then the fascinating world of music will unfold before you.

◄ STAFF ►   Music is written on a *staff* (or *stave*) consisting of five lines and four spaces.

```
5th  LINE _____
4th  LINE _____ 4th  SPACE _____
3rd  LINE _____ 3rd  SPACE _____
2nd  LINE _____ 2nd  SPACE _____
1st  LINE _____ 1st  SPACE _____
```

Musical sounds or *tones* are indicated by symbols called *notes,* and are named after the first seven letters of the alphabet — A B C D E F G. These seven letters must be repeated endlessly to encompass the entire range of musical sound.

The letter-names of the five *lines* are :   The letter-names of the four *spaces* are :

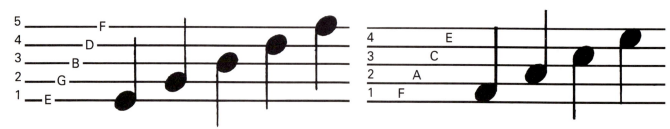

A note has the same letter-name as the line or space that it is written on, and its *pitch,* the height or depth of a tone, is determined by the note's position in, above, or below the staff.

◄ LEGER LINES ►   Since the staff cannot contain all of the notes of the musical system, short lines are added when the pitch of a musical sound is above or below the staff. These extra lines are called *leger lines* and notes are placed on or between them.

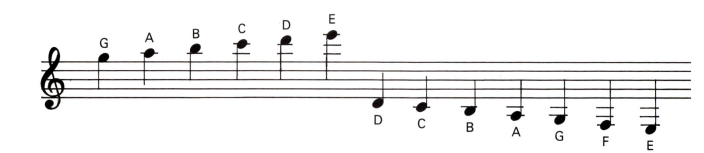

◄ CLEF ► This sign is the *treble clef* or *G clef,* and music embracing the entire range of the guitar is written in this clef. Originally the sign was written smaller — the Gothic letter G was used to establish the pitch of the G note on a four-line staff ...... — today, even though the modern treble clef is larger, the lower part of the sign still circles around the second line or the G line.

Music written for the guitar *sounds* one octave lower than the way it is written.

◄ NOTES ►   (SYMBOLS THAT INDICATE MUSICAL SOUNDS)

Each type of *note* indicates the length of its sound — its value.

STEM ← → FLAG (tail)

HEAD ←

TYPES OF NOTES

WHOLE NOTE	HALF NOTE	QUARTER NOTE	EIGHTH NOTE
semibreve	*minim*	*crotchet*	*quaver*
RECEIVES 4 BEATS	RECEIVES 2 BEATS	RECEIVES 1 BEAT	RECEIVES ½ BEAT
Count — 1 2 3 4	Count — 1 2	Count — 1	Count — for two notes

♪ ♪ = ♫
(½ + ½)   1 and

◄ REST ►   (SIGN MEANING A PERIOD OF SILENCE)

There is an equivalent *rest sign* for each note value.

TYPES OF RESTS

WHOLE REST	HALF REST	QUARTER REST	EIGHTH REST
(hangs down from line)	(lies on line)		
RECEIVES 4 BEATS	RECEIVES 2 BEATS	RECEIVES 1 BEAT	RECEIVES ½ BEAT
Count — 1 2 3 4	Count — 1 2	Count — 1	

◄ **BARS** ► (VERTICAL LINES THAT DIVIDE THE STAFF INTO MEASURES)

All music is divided into parts called *measures,* and vertical lines or *bars* are used on the staff to divide one measure from another. *Double bars* are used to signify that a section or strain of music is completed —*fine* (the end).

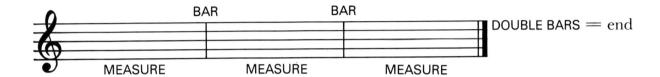

◄ **TIME SIGNATURE** ► Music is made up of *counts* or *beats,* and each measure normally receives an equal number of beats. To indicate the number of beats in each measure, a *time signature* is placed on the staff at the beginning of each musical selection. Time signatures are easy to read : the *upper* number tells you how many beats or counts there are in each measure, and the *lower* number tells you the type of note that receives one beat.

THIS SIGN **4/4** INDICATES FOUR-FOUR TIME

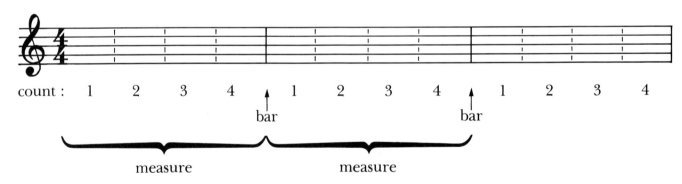

C signifies "COMMON TIME" and means the same as **4/4** = beats in a measure (4)
4/4 = type of note receiving one beat
(quarter note)

THIS SIGN **3/4** INDICATES THREE-FOUR TIME

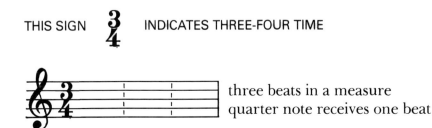

three beats in a measure
quarter note receives one beat

count :   1   2   3

THIS SIGN INDICATES TWO-FOUR TIME

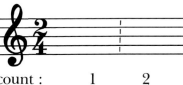

two beats in a measure
quarter note receives one beat

count :   1   2

◄ HOW TO COUNT TIME ►

count : 1   2   3   4   1   2   3   4   1   2   3   4   1 and   2 and   3   4

1   2   3   4   1   2   3   4   1   2   3   4   1 and   2 and   3   4

◄ DOTTED NOTES ►   Whenever a dot (•) is placed after a note, the value of that note
is increased by one-half. (A dot placed after a rest increases its value by one-half.)

DOTTED HALF NOTES

count :   1   2   3   1   2   3

$$\textstyle\unicode{x1D15E} + \cdot = \unicode{x1D15E}.$$

2 + 1 =   3 COUNTS

DOTTED QUARTER NOTES

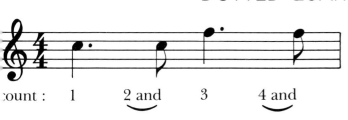

count :   1   2 and   3   4 and

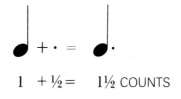

$$\quarternote + \cdot = \quarternote.$$

1 + ½ =   1½ COUNTS

17

◄ REPEAT MARKS ► Double dots (:) placed beside the double bars indicate that the music is to be *repeated* — played again from the beginning.

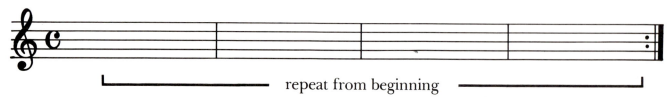

— repeat from beginning —

If there are two sets of double bars with double dots, only the music *between them* is to be repeated.

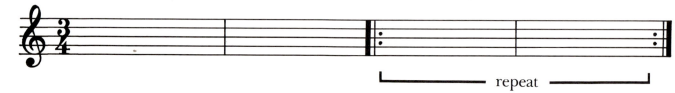

— repeat —

Frequently, there will be two endings for a musical strain or selection — play the piece through ending 1 to the double dots, repeat the measures indicated, then skip ending 1 and finish the piece by playing ending 2.

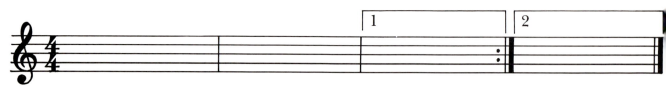

DYNAMICS

Dynamics — signs indicating how soft or loud the music is to be played — appear *below* the staff throughout the musical composition and are placed wherever there is a change in volume. The principal dynamics are :

p soft (piano)   *mf* moderately loud (mezzo-forte)   *f* loud (forte)   *ff* very loud (fortissimo)

TEMPO MARKS

Tempo is the *rate of speed* at which a musical composition is to be played, and tempo marks are placed *above* the staff at the beginning of a composition or a piece. Among the most common tempos are :

LENTO (slow)
ANDANTE (moderately slow, walking)
MODERATO (moderately)

ALLEGRO (fast, happy)
PRESTO (very fast)

The following words indicate *tempo variations* and appear like signposts throughout a musical composition.

accelerando (accel.) becoming faster
rallentando (rall.) slowing down

ritenuto (rit.) hold the movement momentarily
a tempo return to the original tempo

(Frequently, *metronome* (M.) settings are indicated at the beginning of a piece.)

Andante   M. ♩ = 76

f   *p*   rit.

Segovia was once asked by a young beginner of classical guitar : "Maestro, what do you suggest that I consider about interpretation?"

Maestro answered : *"Interpretation should be like life — an explosion of freedom..."*

21

COMPREHENSIVE CHART OF TIME VALUES

notes		beats	rests		beats
○	WHOLE NOTE (semibreve)	4	▬	WHOLE REST (semibreve rest)	4
𝅗𝅥.	DOTTED HALF NOTE	3	▬•	DOTTED HALF REST	3
𝅗𝅥	HALF NOTE (minim)	2	▬	HALF REST (minim rest)	2
♩.	DOTTED QUARTER NOTE	1½	𝄽•	DOTTED QUARTER REST	1½
♩	QUARTER NOTE (crotchet)	1	𝄽	QUARTER REST (crotchet rest)	1
♪.	DOTTED EIGHTH NOTE	¾	𝄾•	DOTTED EIGHTH REST	¾
♪	EIGHTH NOTE (quaver)	½	𝄾	EIGHTH REST (quaver rest)	½
♬	SIXTEENTH NOTE	¼	𝄿	SIXTEENTH REST	¼

(4 sixteenth notes) ♬♬ = ♩ (1 quarter note)

TRIPLET

A *triplet* is a group of three notes to be performed in the place of two of the same value, indicated by a 3 and usually by a slur.

(3 half notes = 1 whole note)   (3 quarter notes = 1 half note)   (3 eighth notes = 1 quarter note)

the fingerboard

The distance from one fret to the next fret, up or down the fingerboard, is a *half step*.

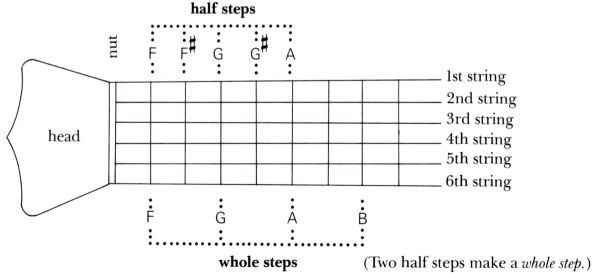

whole steps   (Two half steps make a *whole step*.)

how to read diagrams

The six vertical lines of the diagram represent the six strings of the guitar.

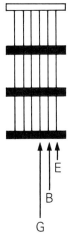

The three *treble strings* are :

1st string (the thinnest string)

2nd string

3rd string

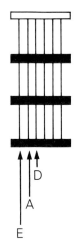

The three *bass strings* are :

4th string

5th string

6th string (the heaviest string)

6 5 4 3 2 1

(1)   The diagrams in this book will simply number the *strings* 6 5 4 3 2 1 as shown.

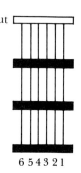

6 5 4 3 2 1

(2)   The horizontal bar at the top of the diagram represents the *nut* of the guitar.

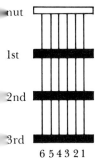

6 5 4 3 2 1

(3)   The heavy horizontal bars represent the *frets* of the guitar and are numbered to the left of the diagram.

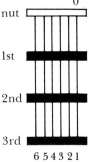

6 5 4 3 2 1

(4)   The 0 at the top of the diagram indicates that the string it is above is to be played *open* (not fingered).

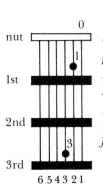

6 5 4 3 2 1

(5)   The black dot indicates the *note* that is to be sounded and where the finger is to be placed. The number to the right of the black dot indicates the *correct finger* to be used.

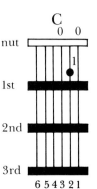

6 5 4 3 2 1

(6)   When two or more tones are to be sounded simultaneously the name of the *chord* is placed above the diagram.

23

how to tune the guitar

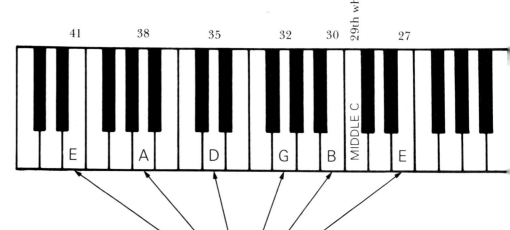

The *easiest method* of tuning the guitar is with a piano. The six *open* strings of the guitar are the same pitch or tone as the six notes shown on the piano keyboard in the illustration.

If you don't know where middle C is, start from the extreme right side of the piano keyboard and count toward the left (white keys only) to the twenty-ninth white key. (This is true of a full-sized piano of seven and one-half octaves. If your piano has a smaller, seven-octave keyboard, it will be the twenty-seventh white key.)

Adjust each string carefully until it agrees with its corresponding piano pitch. Some people use a tuning fork, instead of a piano, to check the pitch.

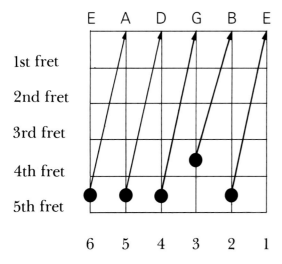

A *second method,* used to tune the guitar when neither a piano nor a tuning fork is available, is relative (approximate) tuning.

1. Tune the (6th) string to E as best you can. The string should not rattle on the frets or be too taut.
2. Press down the 5th fret of the 6th string to get correct pitch of open A string (5th).
3. Press down the 5th fret of the 5th string to get correct pitch of open D string (4th).
4. Press down the 5th fret of the 4th string to get correct pitch of open G string (3rd).
5. Press down the 4th fret of the 3rd string to get correct pitch of open B string (2nd).
6. Press down the 5th fret of the 2nd string to get correct pitch of open E string (1st).

Check each string and retune where necessary.

...with the guitar nothing is easy...

the guitar strings

All modern guitars use the standard string length of 650 mm. which was established by the Spaniard, Antonio Torres, in the mid-nineteenth century. The string length was an important factor in the development of the guitar because it not only determined the size and proportion of the guitar body, but determined the length of the fingerboard as well.

The early classical guitar was strung with three treble strings of fine quality gut and three bass strings of silk wound with yellow or white wire. Today, nylon mono-filament is used for the three treble strings and nylon wound with fine wire is used for the three bass strings. The nylon guitar strings, first made for Andrés Segovia and developed by Albert Augustine in 1947, have many advantages over the old strings, one of which is durability.

When a string breaks or when fret grooves have been made in the wrapping of a bass string, the guitar string must be replaced. You should always use the best available strings on your instrument.

how to hold the guitar

THE CLASSIC PLAYING POSITION

The classic playing position is assumed by the concert guitarist. It is an excellent playing position because it offers the player secure support for the guitar, provides complete freedom of movement for the hands and allows the body to keep a relaxed natural position.

Select an armless chair that is proportioned in height to you and sit forward on it. Rest the front part of your left foot on a flat stool. (*Nature, our mother and sometimes stepmother, learns a great deal from artists. So, I suppose that in a thousand years to come, the predestined guitarist will be born with a longer left leg. In the meanwhile, we will have to use this device.*)

Place your right foot to the right side of the chair and rest it on the toes and ball of the foot.

Put the inward curve of the guitar's body on your left thigh being careful to keep the face of the instrument vertical, *and not pointing the fingerboard too high, but keeping it rather horizontal.*

Lean your body forward slightly to support the guitar against the chest, *for the poetry of the music should resound in your heart.*

Now, rest the right upper arm on the broadest part of the guitar body and allow the rest of the arm to swing free.

Without any other support the guitar will rest securely, almost as an extension of your own body.

Be sure that your left arm and elbow fall comfortably close to your body.

If you assume the correct position now your playing will be persuasive, and will allow your listeners to share your artistic emotions. That is to say, to collaborate with you.

(Ladies must modify the playing position with regard to their legs as shown in the photograph.)

lesson 1
right hand position

Here is a family of fingers —the five brothers in the right hand are named :

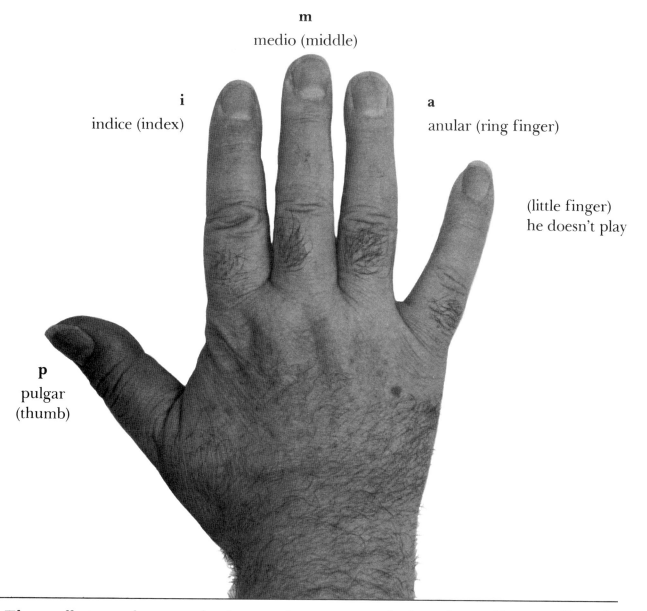

m
medio (middle)

i
indice (index)

a
anular (ring finger)

(little finger)
he doesn't play

p
pulgar
(thumb)

The smallest one does not play because he cannot reach the strings without spoiling the correct position of his mother, the right hand.

We have already stated that the right upper arm rests on the guitar in such a way that it is relaxed, yet can be moved freely. When this happens the right hand bends naturally at the wrist, the fingers cross the strings almost at a right angle and one continuous arch is formed with the wrist, back of the hand and the fingers —*the correct playing position.*

When the right hand is held in the correct playing position the thumb *in action* forms a cross with his brother, the index finger.

There are two principal methods of plucking the strings with the first (**i**), 2nd (**m**) and 3rd (**a**) fingers that utilize this hand position.

The first method is the *apoyando stroke,* also referred to as the rest stroke. (The thumb (**p**) uses this stroke.)

To play the musical notes slide the finger from the plucked string to the next one. Use the apoyando stroke for slow detached notes and slow or rapid scales.

Be careful, don't beat the strings! Pluck the strings and make them sound.

(detached notes)

(apoyando stroke)

The second principal method of plucking the strings with the (**i**), (**m**) and (**a**) fingers is the *tirando stroke,* also known as the free stroke. For the tirando stroke, be sure to curve the finger enough to *clear* the next string. Use the tirando stroke when playing arpeggios, chords or when neighboring strings should vibrate simultaneously.

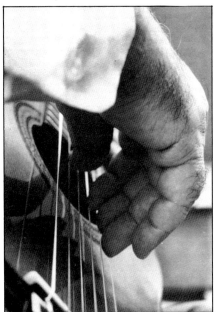

*While the fingers are playing, the thumb (**p**) may follow them by gliding on the bass strings —never anchored on one of them, because the position of the hand is constantly changing.*

OPEN STRINGS — An *open string* is a string that is not pressed by a finger when being plucked. All of the following exercises for open strings should be practiced using the different combinations of fingers : **im**, **mi**, **ma** and **am**.

It is important to practice separately the *apoyando stroke* and the *tirando stroke*, but when you play music you are free to use either kind of stroke depending on the expression you want to bring to the music.

1st string — E (treble)

2nd string — B

4th string — D (use **p** only)

(A circled number indicates the string to be sounded.)

NAIL CARE — It is very important to trim your **right hand nails** correctly for playing the guitar. Their length should be a little longer than the fingertips themselves. The nail edge should be polished and shaped to follow the contour of the fingertip. Obviously, nails that are too long make precise and rapid playing an impossibility, while broken or torn nails may snag or catch on the strings.

lesson 2
left hand position

The brothers in the left hand are called :

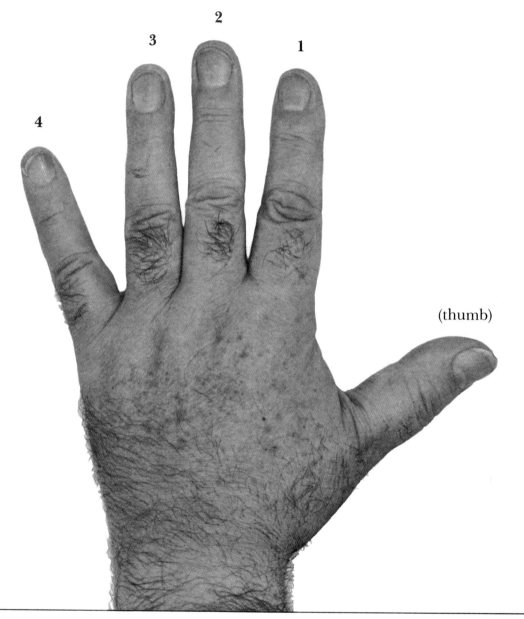

The powerful thumb of the left hand does not play and should remain behind the finger-board. But be careful! He is too inquisitive and likes to look at what his brothers are doing. Forbid him to do so, and oblige him to continue lending his vigor to the other ones. They need his help very much for obtaining a clear and beautiful tone.

We have already learned how to use the right hand fingers. Now I would like to advise you how to employ the ones in the left hand.

1. NAIL CARE — *The left hand nails should be very short to avoid their touching the wood when pressing the musical notes on the strings.*

2.   *The fingers must operate on the strings at right angles, touching them with the fleshy tips.*

3.   *Do not contract the hand, but let it move freely from the wrist without interference of the forearm. Thus the fingers can work with flexibility, attaining great velocity when necessary.*

   I insist in my advice about the thumb. The more he likes to peek out from behind the board, the shorter become the other ones for doing their job. He should place himself behind the fingerboard in the middle of the neck, except when his brother, the index (1), has to press all the strings, in what we call the "barré."

(correct thumb position)

(incorrect thumb position)

   In the bottom of his heart the thumb of the left hand is a little jealous of his brothers; they make the music and receive the praise from the public and the press, and he has in exchange to remain concealed behind the fingerboard.

31

lesson 3
notes on the first string ◀ E ▶

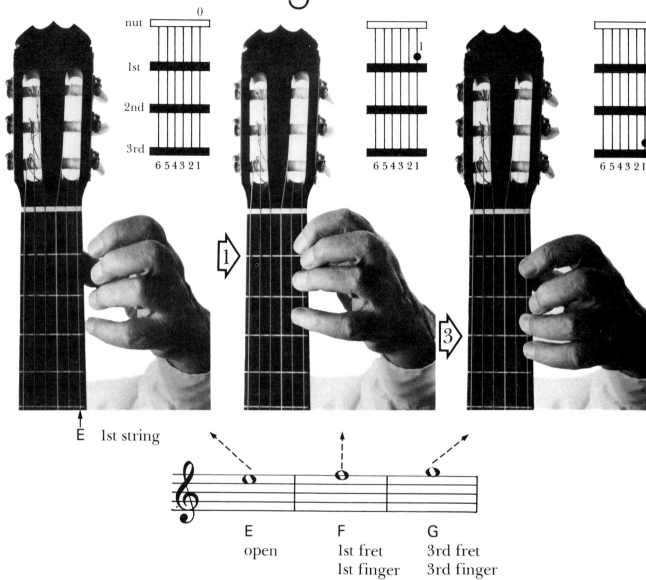

E 1st string

E	F	G
open	1st fret	3rd fret
	1st finger	3rd finger

exercise

E string — fingers 0-1-3

lesson 4
notes on the second string ◀ B ▶

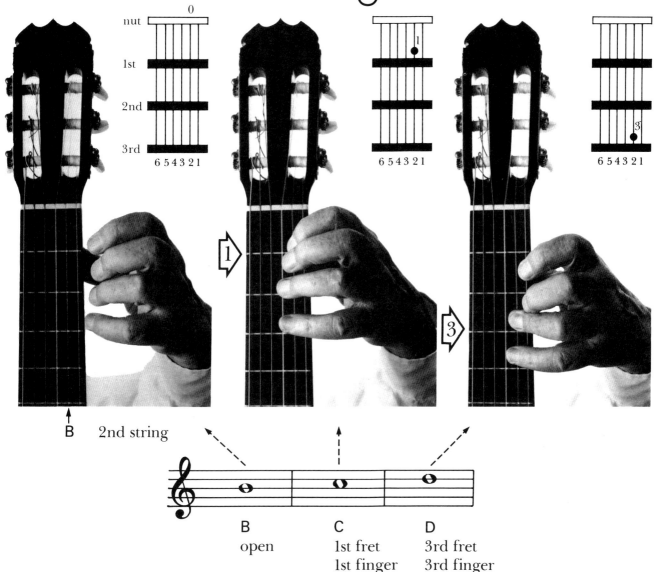

B 2nd string

B	C	D
open	1st fret	3rd fret
	1st finger	3rd finger

exercise

B string — fingers 0-1-3

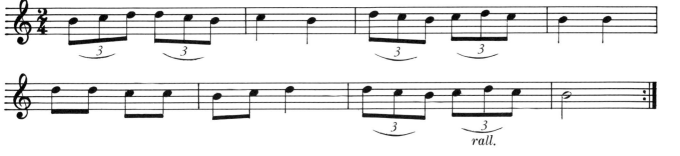

lesson 5
notes on the third string ◀ G ▶

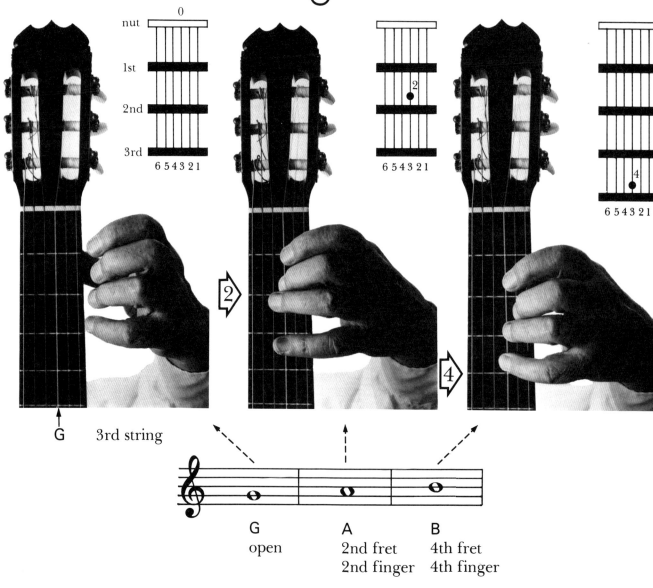

G — 3rd string

G
open

A
2nd fret
2nd finger

B
4th fret
4th finger

exercise

G string — fingers 0-2-4

lesson 6
notes on the fourth string ◄ D ►

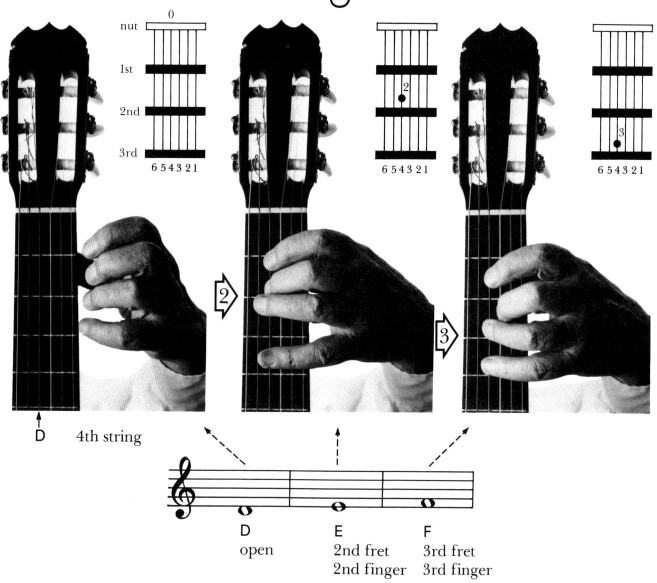

D 4th string

D
open

E
2nd fret
2nd finger

F
3rd fret
3rd finger

exercise

D string — fingers 0-2-3

lesson 7
notes on the fifth string ◀ A ▶

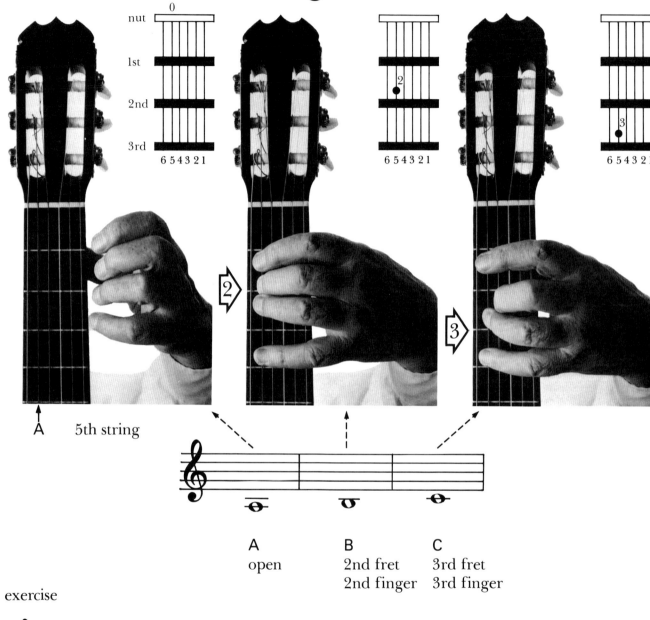

A	B	C
open	2nd fret	3rd fret
	2nd finger	3rd finger

exercise

A string — fingers 0-2-3

lesson 8
notes on the sixth string ◀ E ▶

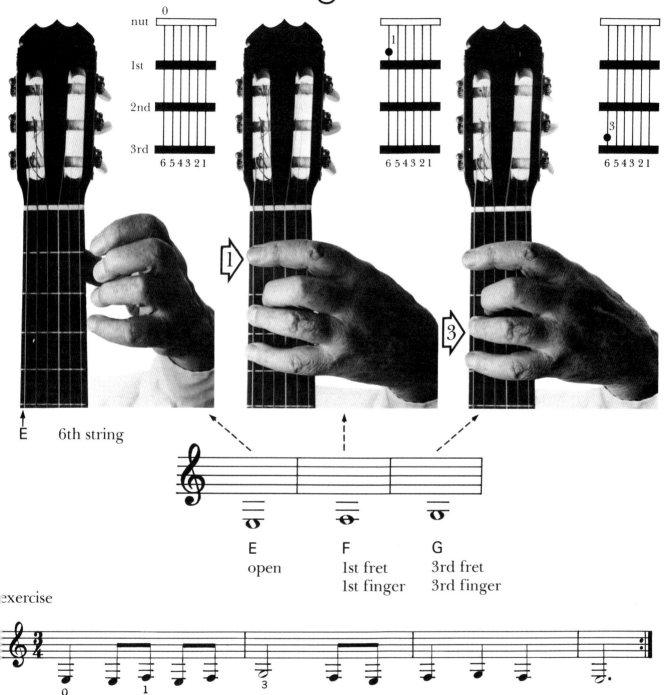

E   6th string

E   F   G
open   1st fret   3rd fret
           1st finger 3rd finger

exercise

E string (bass) — fingers 0-1-3

lesson 9

◄ STEPS ►   A *half step* (semitone) is the distance from a given tone to the next higher or lower tone. The distance of a half step on the guitar is *one fret*.

A *whole step* consists of two half steps — on the guitar the distance of a whole step is *two frets*.
(SEE THE FINGERBOARD ILLUSTRATION ON PAGE 22)

◄ CHROMATICISM ►   Chromaticism is a progression of tones or sounds that move by a half step. For this purpose we use signs referred to as *accidentals* :

♯ sharps   The sharp sign placed before a note *raises* its pitch a half step or one fret for the measure in which it appears.

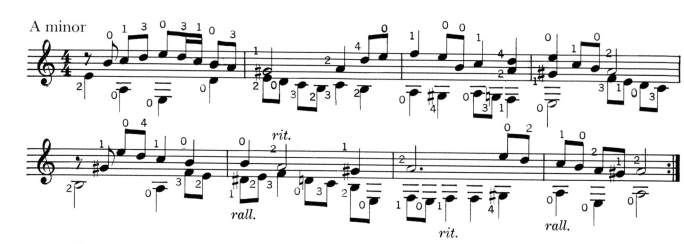

♭ flats   The flat sign placed before a note *lowers* its pitch a half step or one fret for the measure in which it appears. The sign (♭) placed on the staff at the beginning of the following study indicates the note B is *always* played B flat throughout the composition. (When a note is always to be played as a sharp it is indicated in the same way, but with the sharp sign.)

♮ naturals   The natural sign placed before a note *cancels* a previous sharp or flat and restores a note to its normal pitch. (⌒ =*tie* play first note, hold for time duration of two notes)

key signatures — scales

Key signature — the sharps or flats appearing at the beginning of each staff, indicating the scale and the key of the composition. There are, however, always two keys, one major and one minor, having the same key signature (relative keys) and the decision between these two possibilities has to be made from the music itself. You will learn more about this with advanced studies.

Remember, sharps or flats shown in the key signature are effective throughout the scale or the piece unless canceled by a natural sign.

Scale — a succession of notes, normally either a whole tone or a half tone apart, arranged in ascending or descending order.

A piece based on the **C major scale** is in the **key of C major.** There are no sharps or flats in the following scale (C major) but a piece in the key of C major may have sharps or flats (accidentals) occurring in it. Extra notes in parentheses have been added for convenience in fingering.

C major

A piece based on the G major scale is in the **key of G major.** The accidental signs in parentheses in the following scale are just reminders that a sharp is shown in the key signature.

G major

The *chromatic scale* is formed exclusively of *half steps.*

(use sharps ascending)

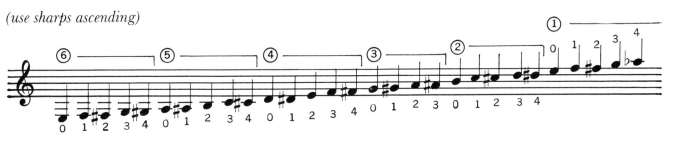

(use flats descending)

NOTE : practice each scale using — **im, mi, ma** and **am** fingering

39

lesson 10
chords — arpeggios

A *chord* is a combination of three or more different notes sounded together. When notes are to be played together as a chord, they are written in a single column.

A succession of single tones :

The same tones as a chord :

A *broken chord* — ARPEGGIO — is the sounding of the notes of a chord in succession instead of simultaneously.

The following illustrations show different ways that a chord may be sounded :

GLISSANDO —— STRUMMING THE CHORD

The p——➤ at the bottom of the diagram indicates that the thumb is to sound the C chord producing arpeggio by sliding the thumb from the 5th to the 1st string.
1) The notes are omitted and the chord name appears instead above the staff.
2) x _ _ _ _ _ _ _ _ _ _ indicates that the left hand fingers should *hold* the notes.

3) The sign … { … indicates *arpeggio*.

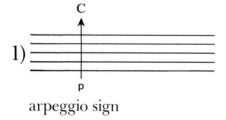

arpeggio sign

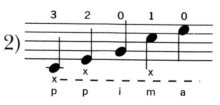

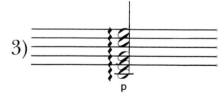

PLUCKING THE CHORD

arpeggio (broken chord)

notes plucked simultaneously
(plucked chord)

STUDY IN CHORDS

Written by JESÚS SILVA for Nicole and George Mendoza

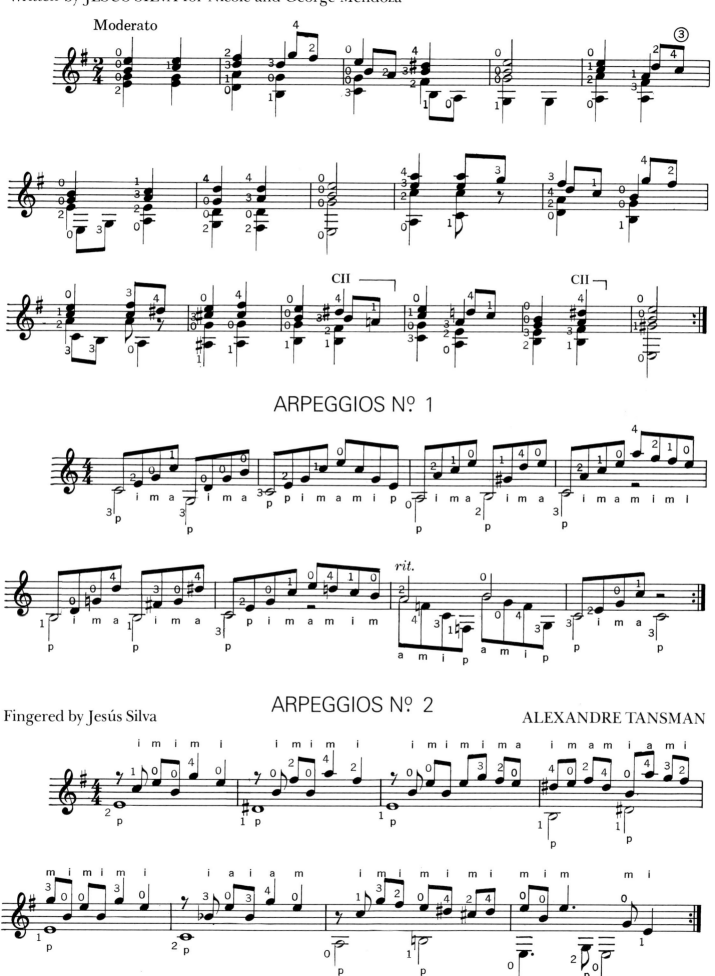

ARPEGGIOS Nº 1

ARPEGGIOS Nº 2

Fingered by Jesús Silva

ALEXANDRE TANSMAN

selected studies

different authors'
little studies for starting
the discipline of the fingers
and the development of
good musical taste!
selected,
revised and fingered
by
andrés segovia

The following group of studies were written by well known masters of the guitar. I have tried to put them in order according to their progressive difficulties.

The guitar is not like the violin, cello, or the piano because through the continuing history of widescale teaching of these latter instruments have passed many, many great masters, whereas the guitar has had relatively few. Fernando Sor *(1778-1839), Mauro* Giuliani *(1781-1829), Dionisio* Aguado *(1784-1849), Napoleon* Coste *(1806-1883) and Francisco Eixea* Tárrega *(1852-1909) were some of the great masters of the guitar; and more recently, Heitor* Villa-Lobos *(1887-1959), whose studies for the guitar are true concert pieces.*

This little exercise was written by **Fernando Sor** *and his purpose was just for teaching how to play the apoyando. But there are also certain notes in it which are to be played with the thumb.*

Fingered and Revised by Andrés Segovia

FERNANDO SOR

Vladimir Bobri *has been a dear friend of mine, almost since my first visit in New York. His love for the guitar has not been surpassed by anybody. In his feelings for that instrument he is two-faced : fond of both flamenco and classical; and he also invents "farsetas" and composes preludes, studies and alluring pieces in orthodox style, like the ones that follow.*

Andante

Lento

Robert de Visée *(1650-1722) was guitarist and lutenist of the Court of Louis XIV and teacher of the Dauphin. He dedicated to the King a group of delicate compositions. Among the praises he included in his dedication there was a charming one —"you, sir, whose hands have the same dexterity for playing the guitar as for giving to the army the order for battle…"*

MINUET

ROBERT DE VISÉE

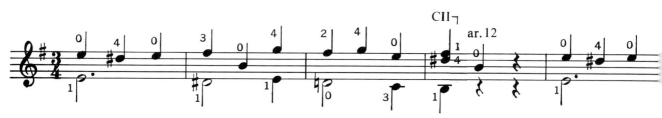

This piece was composed by **Napoleon Coste,** *a pupil of Fernando Sor. It is a little more complicated, but I think that the student will have enough determination to master it.*

NAPOLEON COSTE

A Russian poet sent once a delicious madrigal of two verses to his sweetheart telling her : "Dearest, pardon me, I had no time to make it shorter…" My "Brief Anecdote" could have the same significance.

BRIEF ANECDOTE
(popular song)

ANDRÉS SEGOVIA

< crescendo, means *grow louder*   > diminuendo, means *grow softer*

This little piece was composed by **Dionisio Aguado** *and it provides a useful lesson in beginning to play double notes in thirds.*

DIONISIO AGUADO

This is a small lesson in chords that I composed many years ago.

STUDIES OF CHORDS

ANDRÉS SEGOVIA

The hold sign 𝄐 (fermata = pause) placed over or under a note or rest, indicates the *prolonging* of its timc value.

This lesson was composed by **Napoleon Coste** *under the influence of Fernando Sor. I think that this influence is the reason for its charming, melodic and poetical tempo.*

NAPOLEON COSTE

My head was made in stone —not by God, who wa
very generous creating it —but by the magnificen
sculptor Enrique Perez Comendador.

NAPOLEON COST

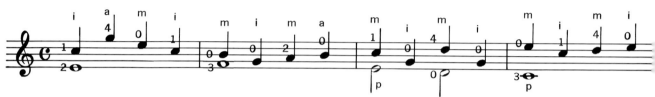

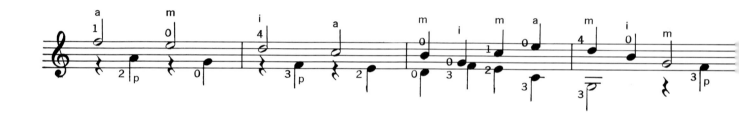

Hipolito Hidalgo de Caviedes —painter. The angel playing the guitar was a gift from him to my boy, Carlos Andrés.

DIONISIO AGUADO

This piece was written by Niccolò Paganini (1784-1840), the greatest violinist of his time and model for the technique of the same instrument in the ensuing centuries.

Little piece written by N. Paganini for the guitar

NICCOLÒ PAGANINI

dictionary
of the guitar and related musical terms

accelerando
— (accel.) gradually increasing in speed; becoming faster

accidentals
— signs relating to or indicating sharps, flats or naturals

accompaniment
— a portion of the musical text designed to serve as background for other musical parts

allegro
— a tempo term indicating to go fast; happy

andante
— a tempo term indicating to go moderately slow such as "going" or "walking"

apoyando stroke
— (rest stroke) a principal method of plucking the strings of the guitar with the thumb and the 1st, 2nd and 3rd fingers of the right hand

arpeggio
— the sounding of the notes of a chord in succession instead of simultaneously

artistry
— artistic workmanship that produces high quality

ascend
— to rise in pitch; pass from any tone to a higher one

a tempo
— return to the original tempo

bar
— also called bar line — vertical line drawn through the staff to mark off measures

barré
— a way of pressing all six strings on the same fret of the guitar simultaneously with the 1st finger of the left hand

beat
— to mark (time) by strokes, as with the hand or a metronome : *count* 1 2 3 4 etc.

bridge
— a thin support that raises the strings of a musical instrument above the sounding board

chord
— a combination of three or more different notes played together

chromatic scale
— a scale progressing entirely by semi-tones or half steps

chromaticism
— the use of raised or lowered notes, instead of the normal degrees of the scale; chromaticism is a progression of tones or sounds that move by a half step — for this purpose accidentals are used :
sharp (♯), flat (♭) and natural (♮)

clef
— a symbol placed upon a staff to indicate the name and pitch of the notes corresponding to its lines and spaces

common time
— (**C**) the same as $\frac{4}{4}$ time

composition
— a piece of music

descend
— to go down in pitch; to pass from any tone to a lower one

diatonic scale
— a scale containing whole steps and half steps; major (also minor) scale

dissonance
— a simultaneous combination of tones conventionally accepted as being in a state of unrest and needing completion; discord

double bar

— two vertical lines placed together on a staff indicating the end of a piece of music or a sub-division of it

duet

— a composition for two instruments or two voices

duration

— the length of time something continues or exists

dynamics

— the signs showing how soft or loud to play the music :
ff very loud; *f* loud; *mf* moderately loud;
pp very soft; *p* soft; *mp* moderately soft

flat

— in musical notation the symbol (♭) placed before a note lowers its pitch a half step

form
— the way music is constructed

half barré

— a way of pressing fewer than six strings on the same fret of the guitar simultaneously with the 1st finger of the left hand

harmony

— any simultaneous combination of musical tones

hold sign

— (⌢) this sign placed over or under a note or rest indicates the prolonging of its time value

instrument

— a contrivance or device for performing musical sounds

interpretation

— the rendering of music so as to bring out the meaning, or to indicate one's particular conception of it

interval

— the difference in pitch between two tones, as between two tones sounded simultaneously (harmonic interval) or between two tones sounded successively (melodic interval)

key

— the principal tonality of a composition : *a symphony in the key of C minor*

leger line

— a short line added when necessary above or below the staff to increase the range of the staff

lento

— a tempo term indicating to go slow

major

— related to a key in which the third note of the scale produces a major third interval

major scale

— a scale containing five whole steps and two half steps; the half steps go between the third and fourth note and between the seventh and eighth note of the scale; the eighth note has the same name as the first, one octave higher; the major scale step pattern is : 1, 1, ½, 1, 1, 1, ½

measure

— the music contained between two bar lines; bar

melody

— the succession of single tones in musical composition, as distinguished from harmony and rhythm

metronome

— (M.M. or M.) a mechanical or electrical instrument that makes repeated clicking sounds at an adjustable pace, used for marking time

minor

— related to a key in which the third note of the scale produces a minor third interval

minor scale

— a scale containing whole steps and half steps; the two forms of the minor scale are : 1. melodic 2. harmonic

moderato
— a tempo term indicating to go moderately

motif

— a distinctive and recurring theme in any musical work

61

music
— an art of sound in time which expresses ideas and emotions in significant forms through the elements of rhythm, melody and harmony

natural
— in musical notation the sign (♮) placed before a note cancels a previous sharp (♯) or flat (♭) and restores a note to its normal pitch

notation
— a special system of graphic symbols and signs used in writing music

note
— a sign or character used to represent a tone, its position and form indicating the pitch and duration of the tone

octave
— the interval embracing eight diatonic tones

open
— a string that is not pressed by a finger when being plucked

part
— a section or fragment of a composition or a complete part of a major musical work such as a movement of a sonata or a suite

piece
— a musical composition

pitch
— the height or depth of a tone

pluck
— to sound (the strings of a musical instrument) by pulling at them with the fingers

position
— any of the places on the fingerboard of a stringed instrument where the fingers press the strings to produce the various pitches

presto
— a tempo term indicating to go very fast; quick movement

rallentando
— (rall.) slowing down

recital
— a musical entertainment given usually by a single performer or by a group of performers

repeat
— two dots placed beside the double bars calling for a passage or a section to be repeated

repertoire
— the list of works which a musician is prepared to perform

rest
— a sign used to designate a period of silence between tones

rhythm
— the pattern of regular or irregular pulses caused in music by the occurrence of strong and weak melodic and harmonic beats

ritenuto
— (rit.) hold the movement momentarily

rudiments
— the elements or first principles of a subject

scale
— a succession of tones ascending or descending according to fixed intervals

semitones
— (half step, half tone) a pitch interval halfway between two whole tones

sharp
— in musical notation the sign (♯) placed before a note raises its pitch a half step

sign
— (symbol) used in musical notation to indicate various musical aspects

signature
— a sign or set of signs at the beginning of a staff to indicate the key or the time of a piece

slur
— an arching line drawn over a group of notes

solo
— performing alone

staff

— (stave) a set of five horizontal lines with the corresponding four spaces between them on which music is written

steps

— a degree (tone or step) of the staff or of the scale

stroke

— a single complete movement which can be repeated

style

— it may refer to the composer's manner of writing, the character of the music itself or to the *style of performance*

suspension

— the prolongation of a tone in one chord into the following chord, usually producing a temporary dissonance

technique

— ability to apply procedures or methods so as to effect a desired result; manner or method of performance

tempo

— relative rate of movement of a musical composition

tempo marks

— indications of the speed of a composition or a piece; proceeding from the slowest to the fastest, these are :

largo–very slow, broad, stately

. ♩ = 42 (example of a metronome setting indicating 42 quarter notes are played during one minute)

lento–slow

adagio–slower than andante

andante–moderately slow and even, walking

andantino–faster than andante

moderato–moderately

allegro moderato–moderately fast

allegretto–lively, light

allegro–fast, happy

vivace–faster than allegro

presto–very fast

theme

— a principal melodic subject in a musical composition

theory

— the branch of music which deals with its principles or methods, as distinguished from its practice

tie

— a curved line between two notes of the same pitch — the first note is played and held for the time duration of both — the second note is not played but held

timbre

— quality of the tone; depends upon the quality of the instrument and the skill of the performer; color tone

time

— the general movement of a particular kind of musical composition with reference to its rhythm, metrical structure and tempo

tirando stroke

— (free stroke) a principal method of plucking the strings of the guitar with the 1st, 2nd and 3rd fingers of the right hand

tone

— a musical sound of definite pitch

transposition

— the playing or rewriting of a composition in a key different from the original

triplet

— a group of three notes to be performed in the time of two ordinary notes of the same kind

tune

1. a succession of musical sounds forming an air or melody, with or without the harmony accompanying it
2. (to tune) adjust a musical instrument to a correct or given standard of pitch

vihuela

— a direct predecessor of the guitar

LIBRARY OF CONGRESS CATALOGING IN PUBLICATION DATA

Segovia, Andrés, 1893–
Segovia: my book of the guitar.
SUMMARY: Uses text, photographs, diagrams, and musical
exercises to provide the beginner and intermediate student
with a basic instructional guide to the classical guitar.
  1. Guitar—Methods—Juvenile. 2. Guitar—Methods—
Self-instruction. [1. Guitar—Methods]
I. Mendoza, George. II. Title.
MT801.G8S43   787'.61' 0712   79-10277
ISBN 0-399-20966-2